SHELLS

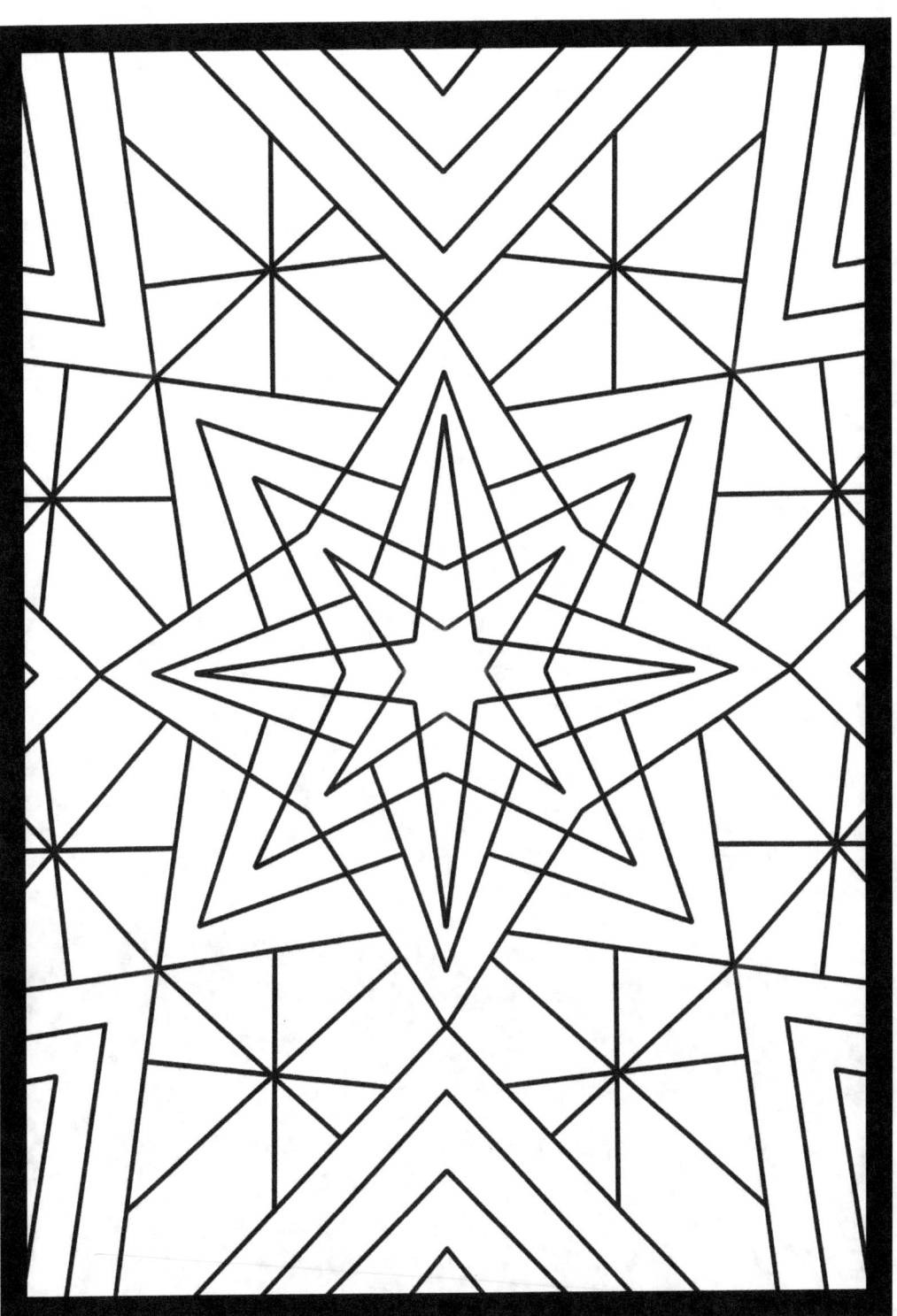

ARIES

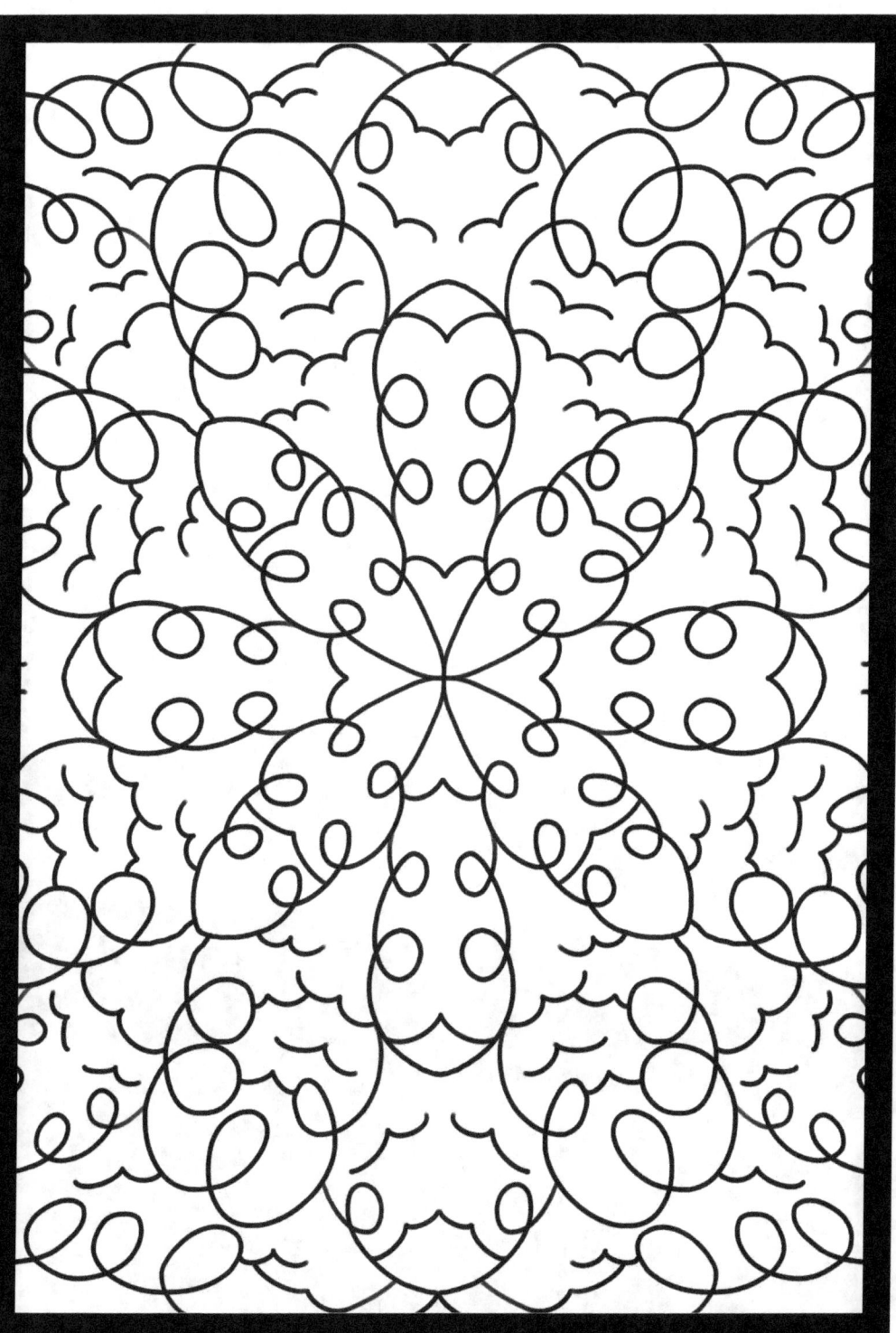

CLOUDS

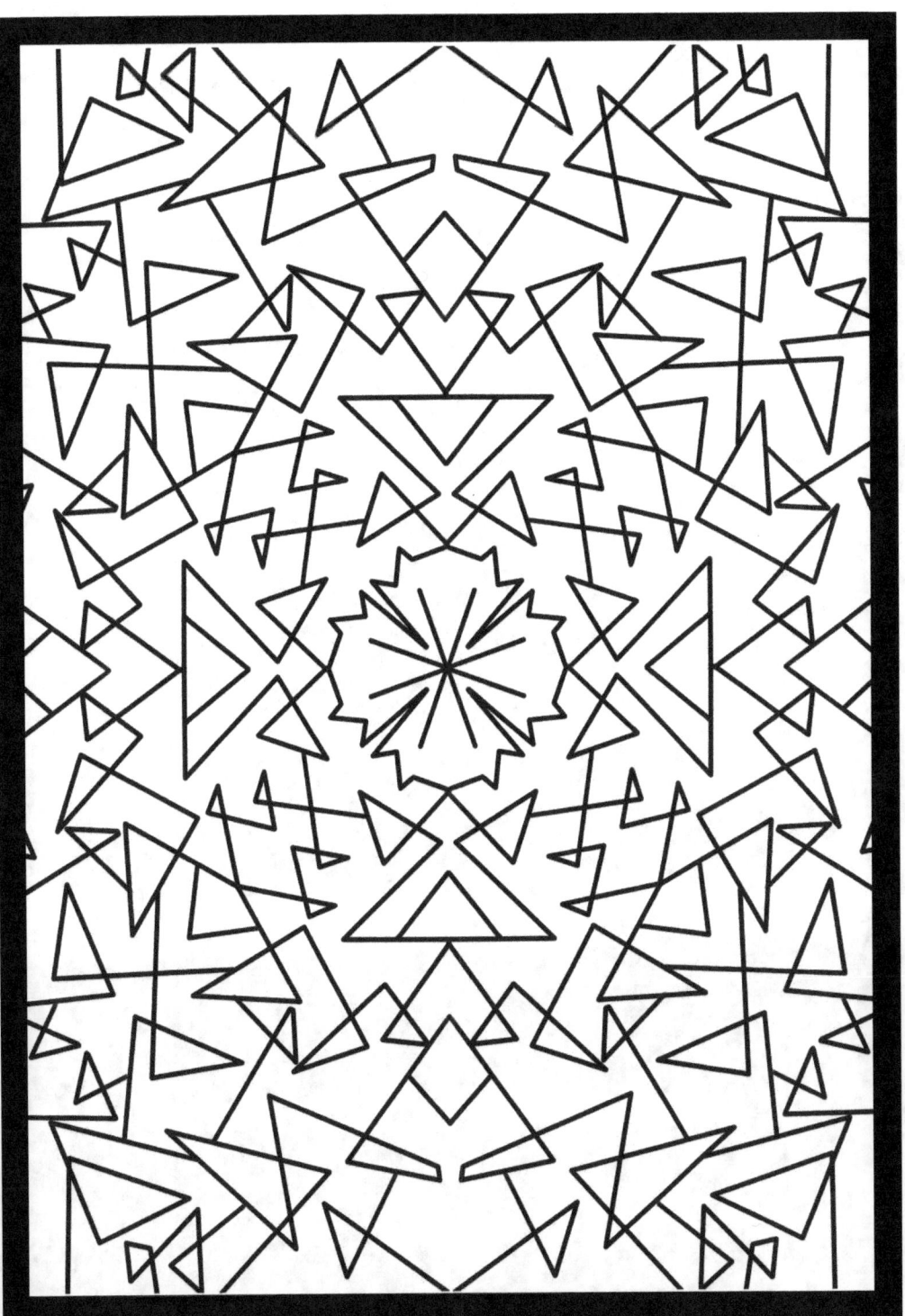
SHARP

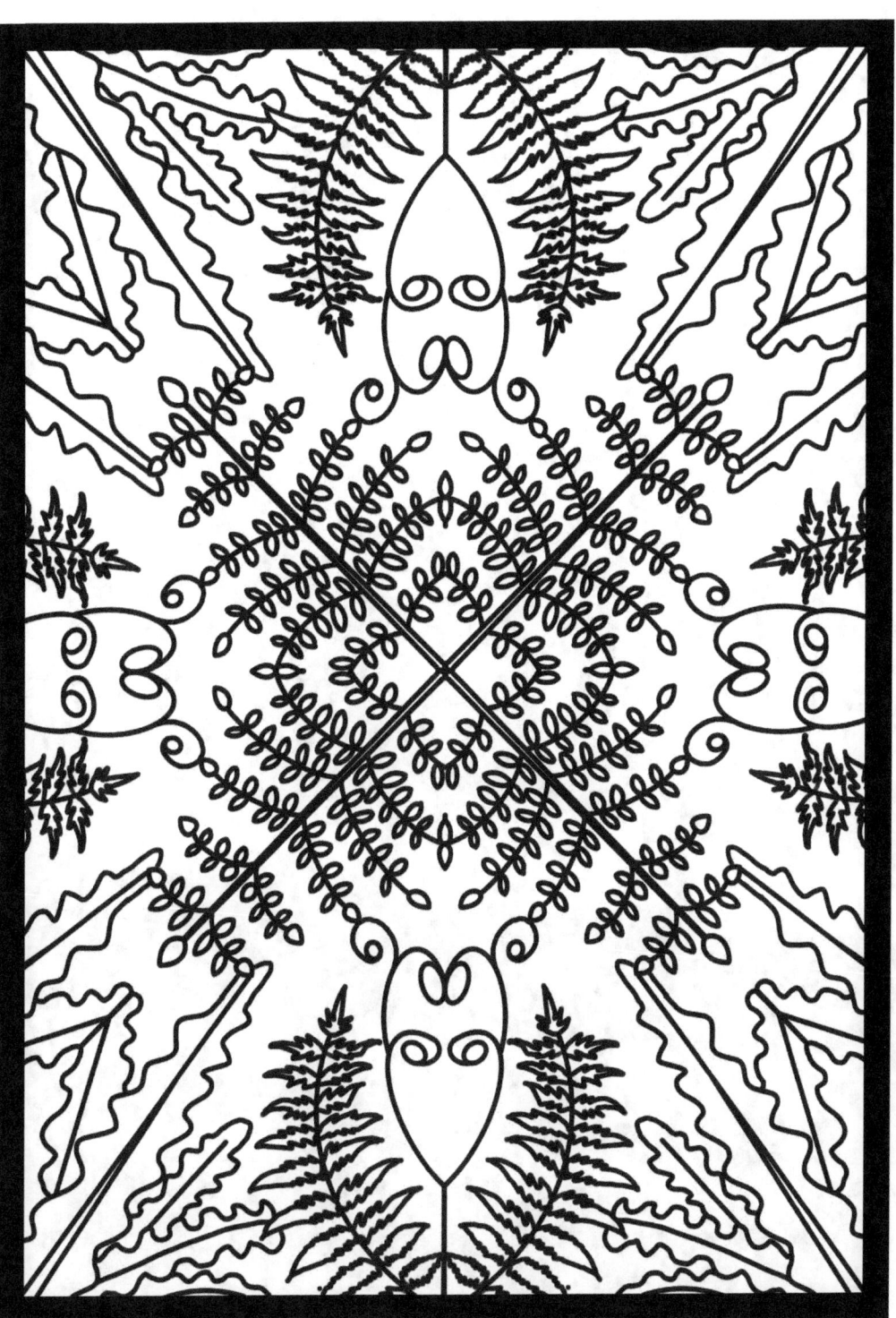

FERNS

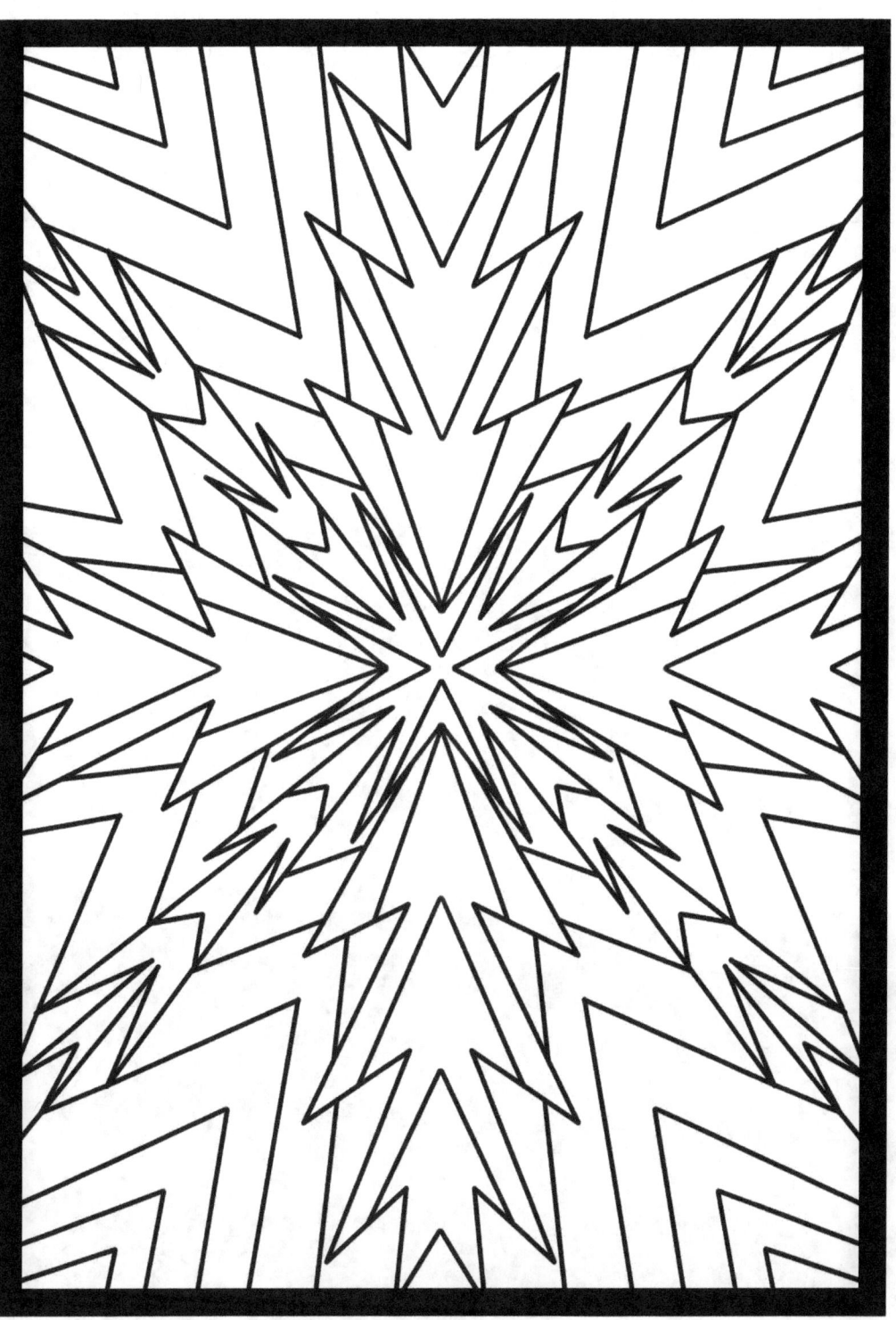
ARROWS

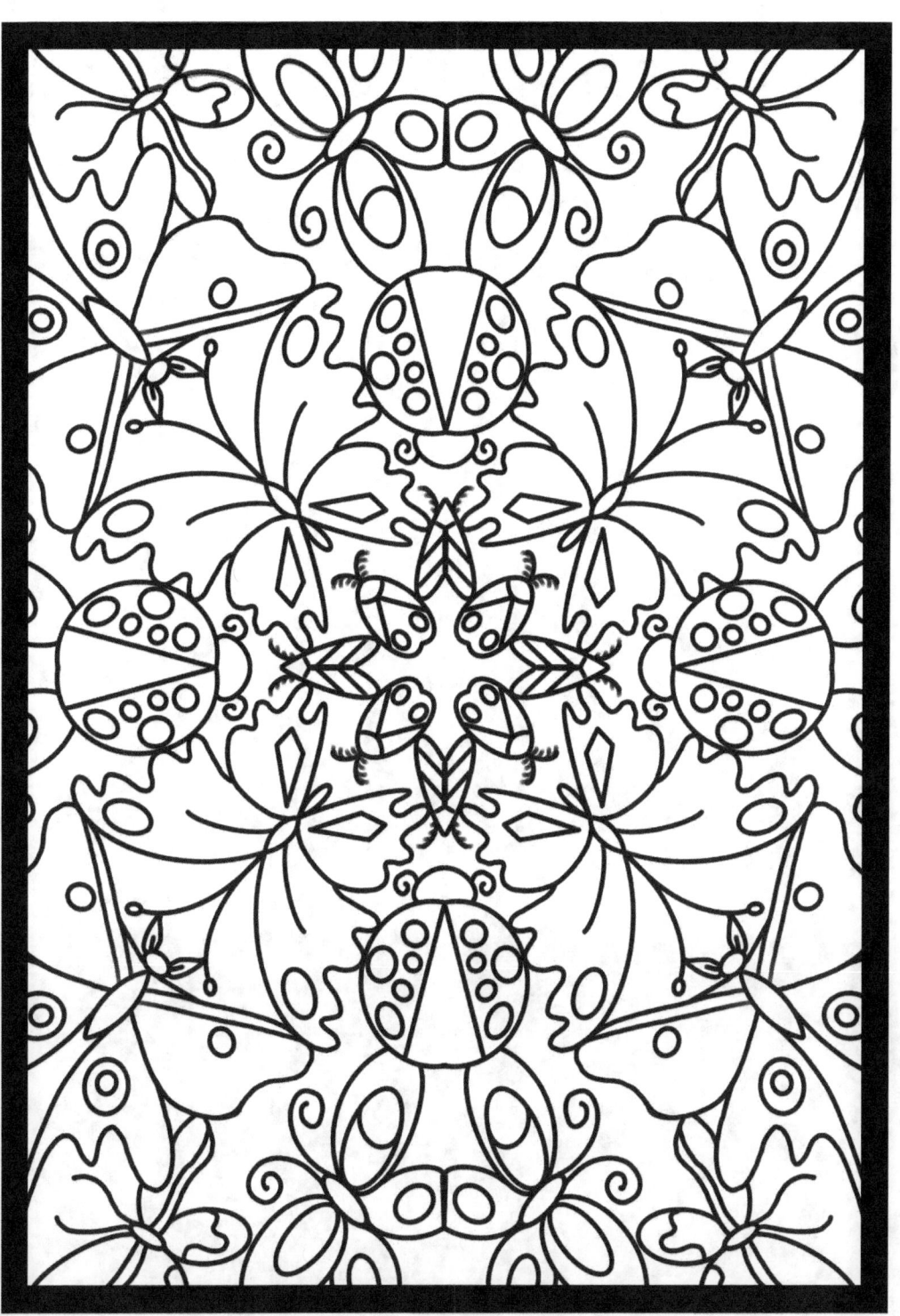

IN TIME BUTTERFLY

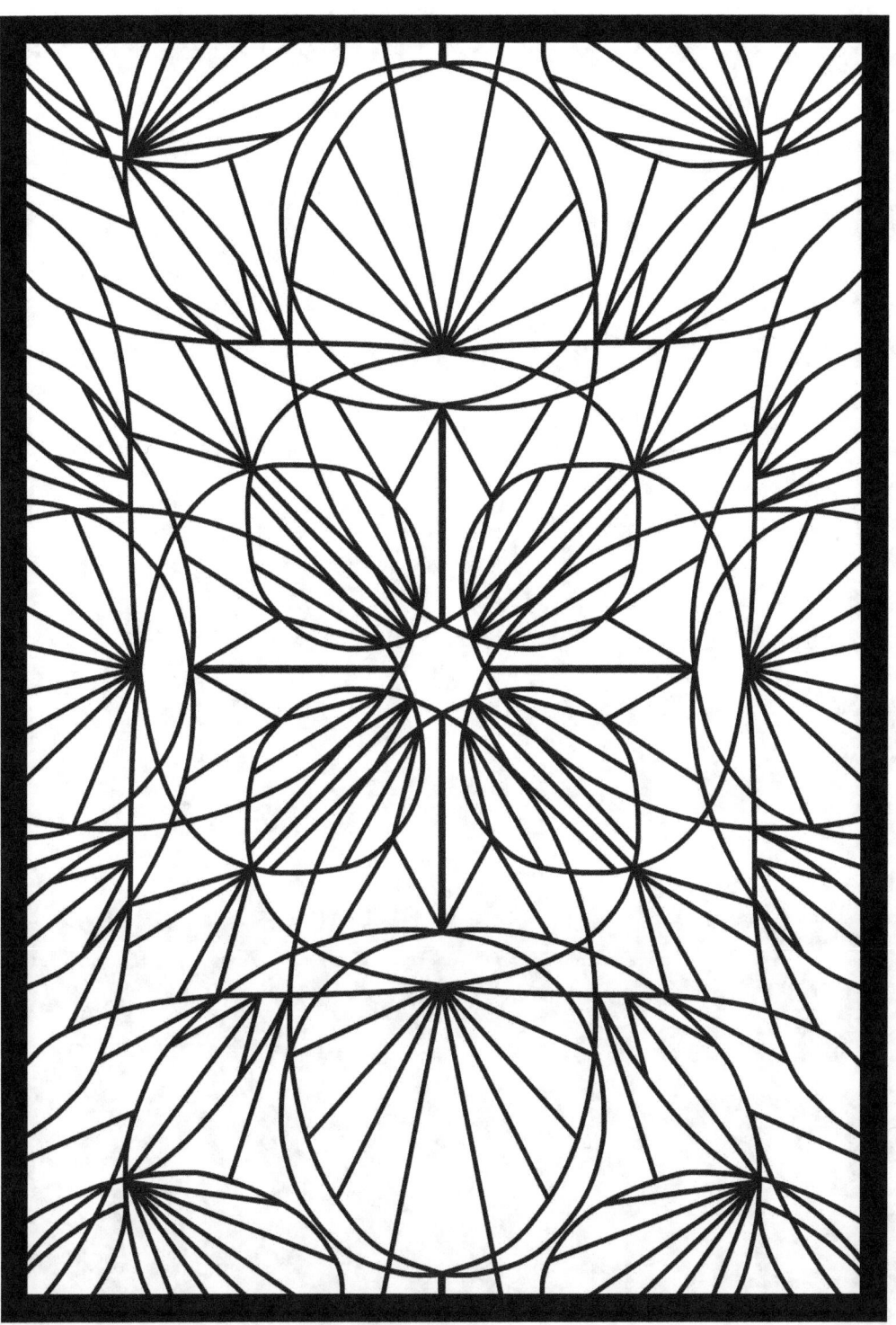

FANS

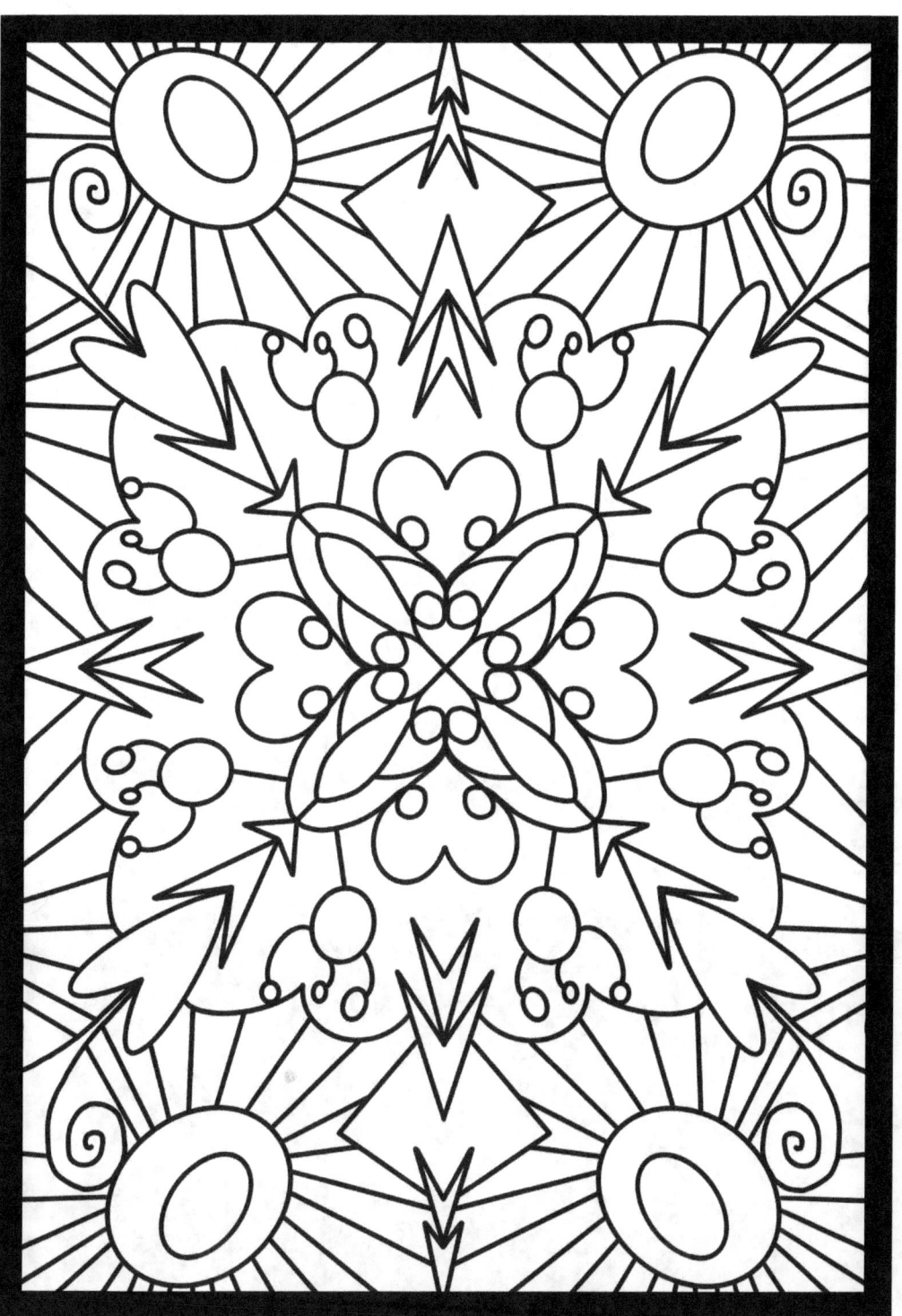

SUNNY DAY

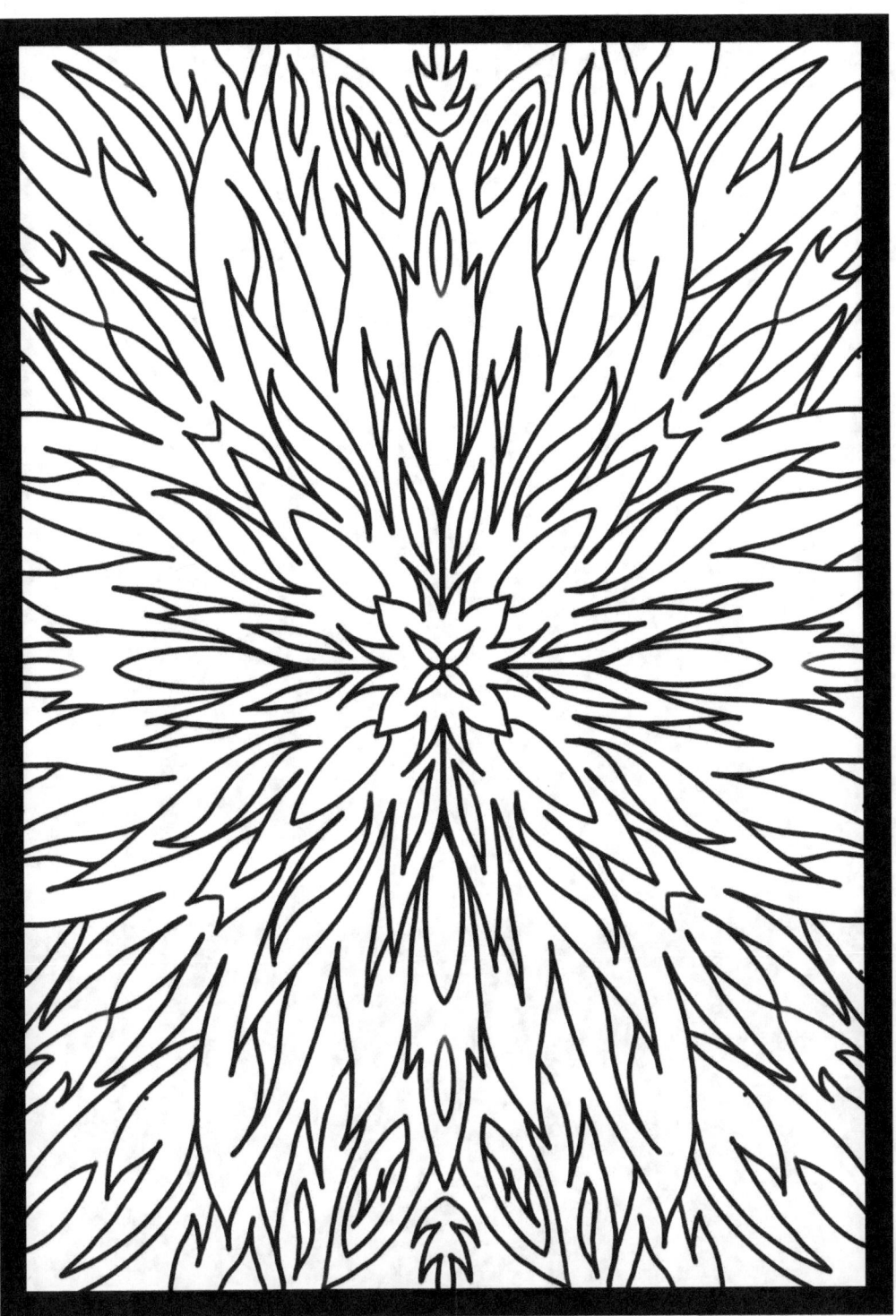

FIRE

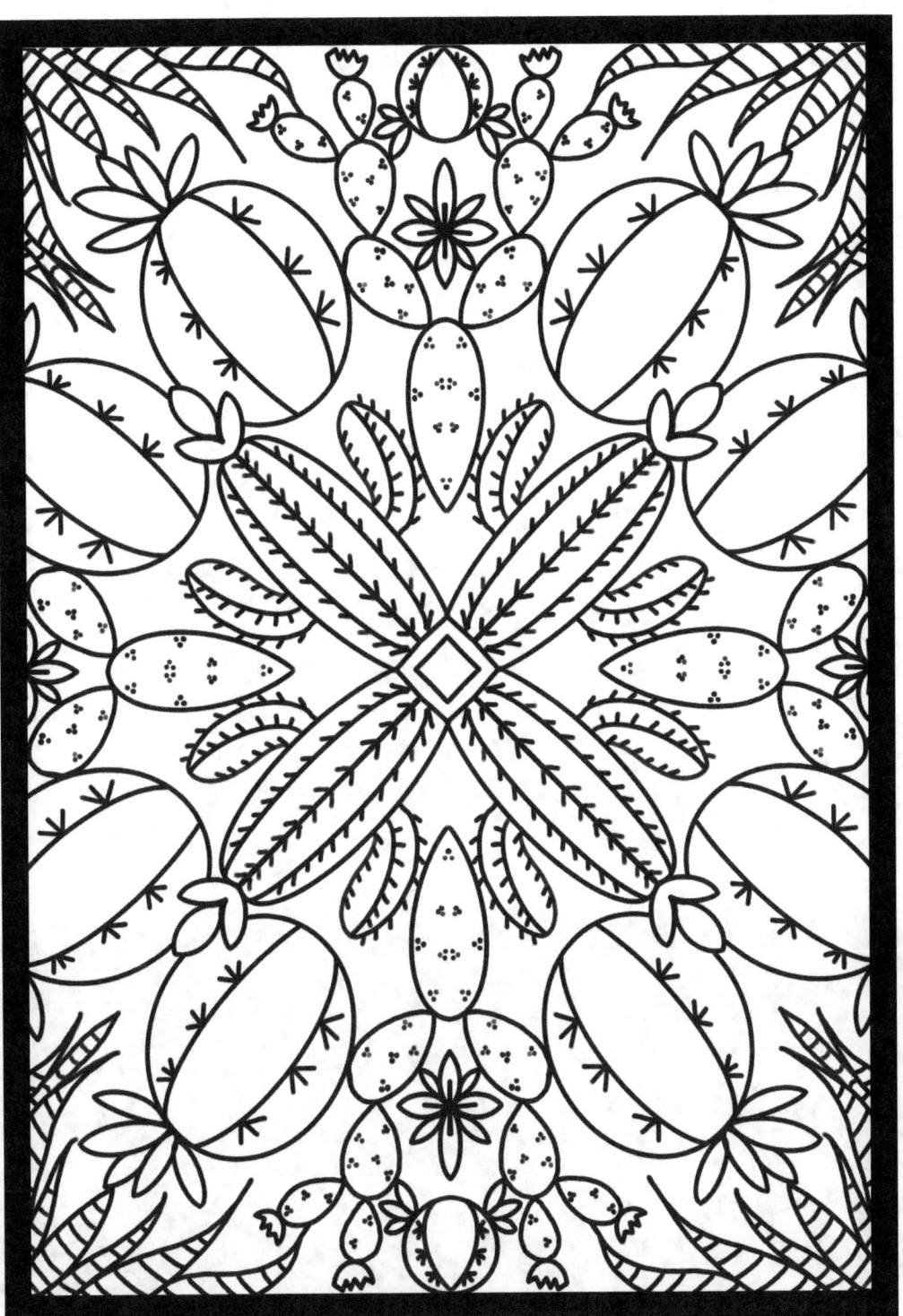

CACTI

SPLASH

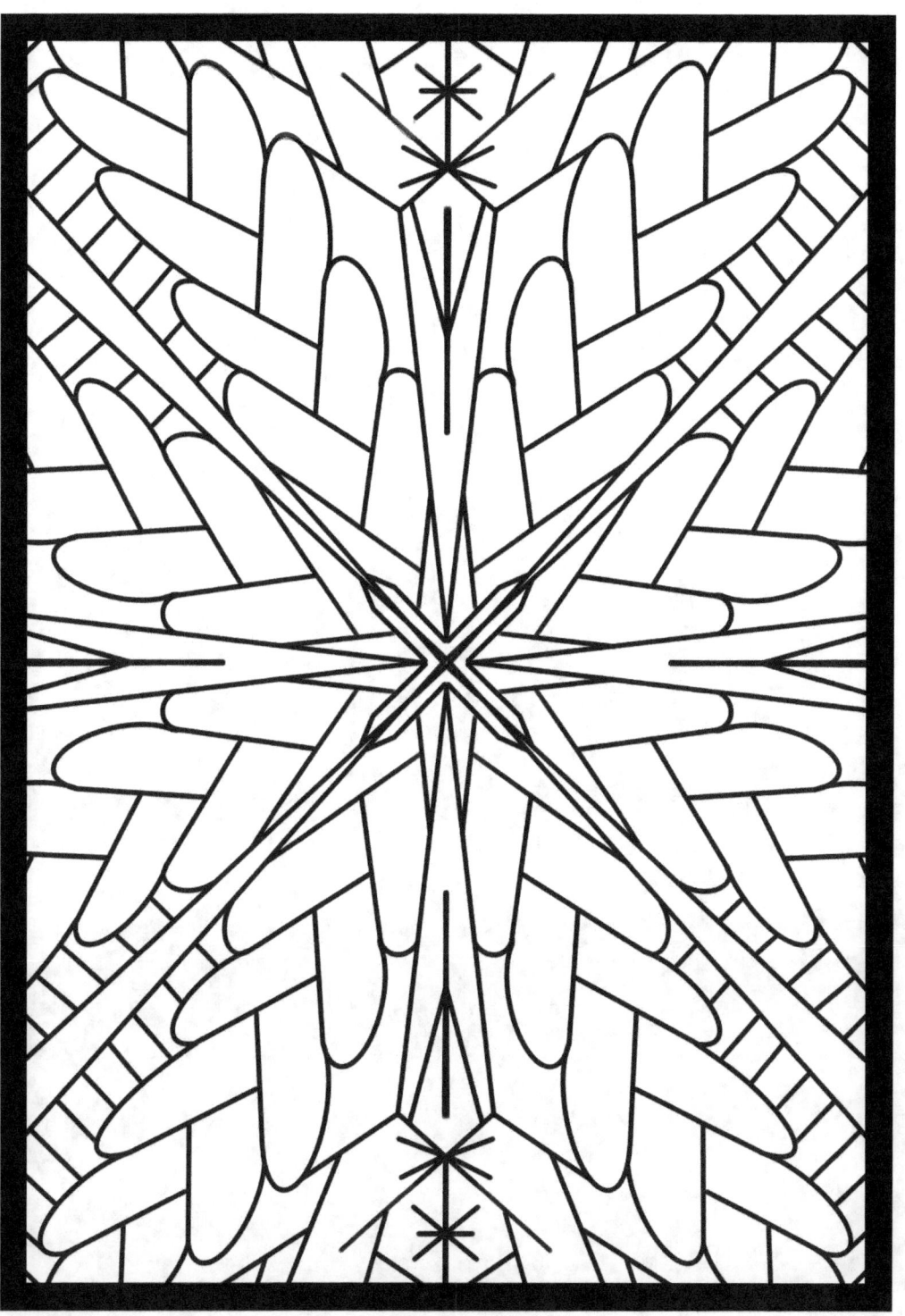

BRAID

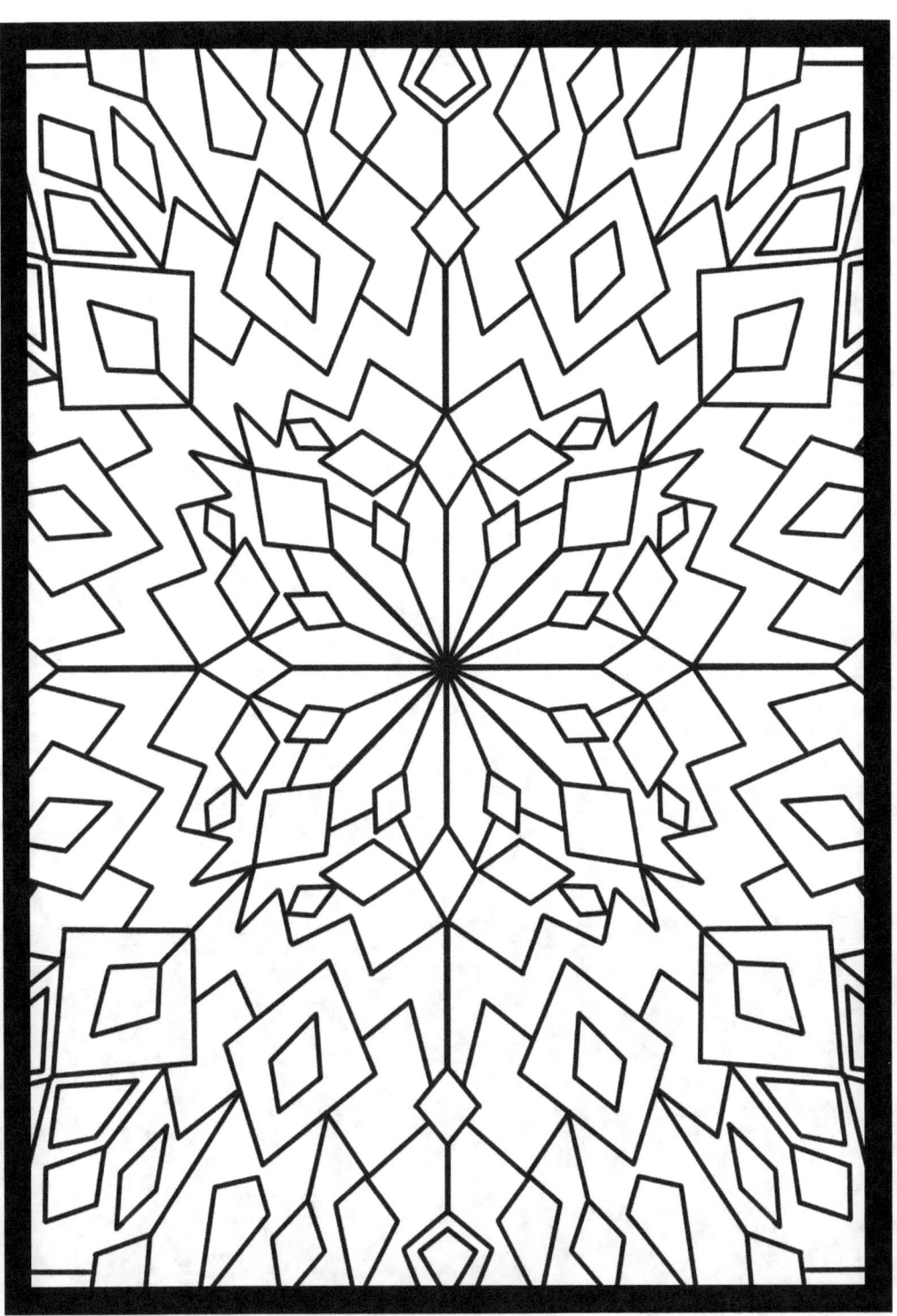

DIAMONDS

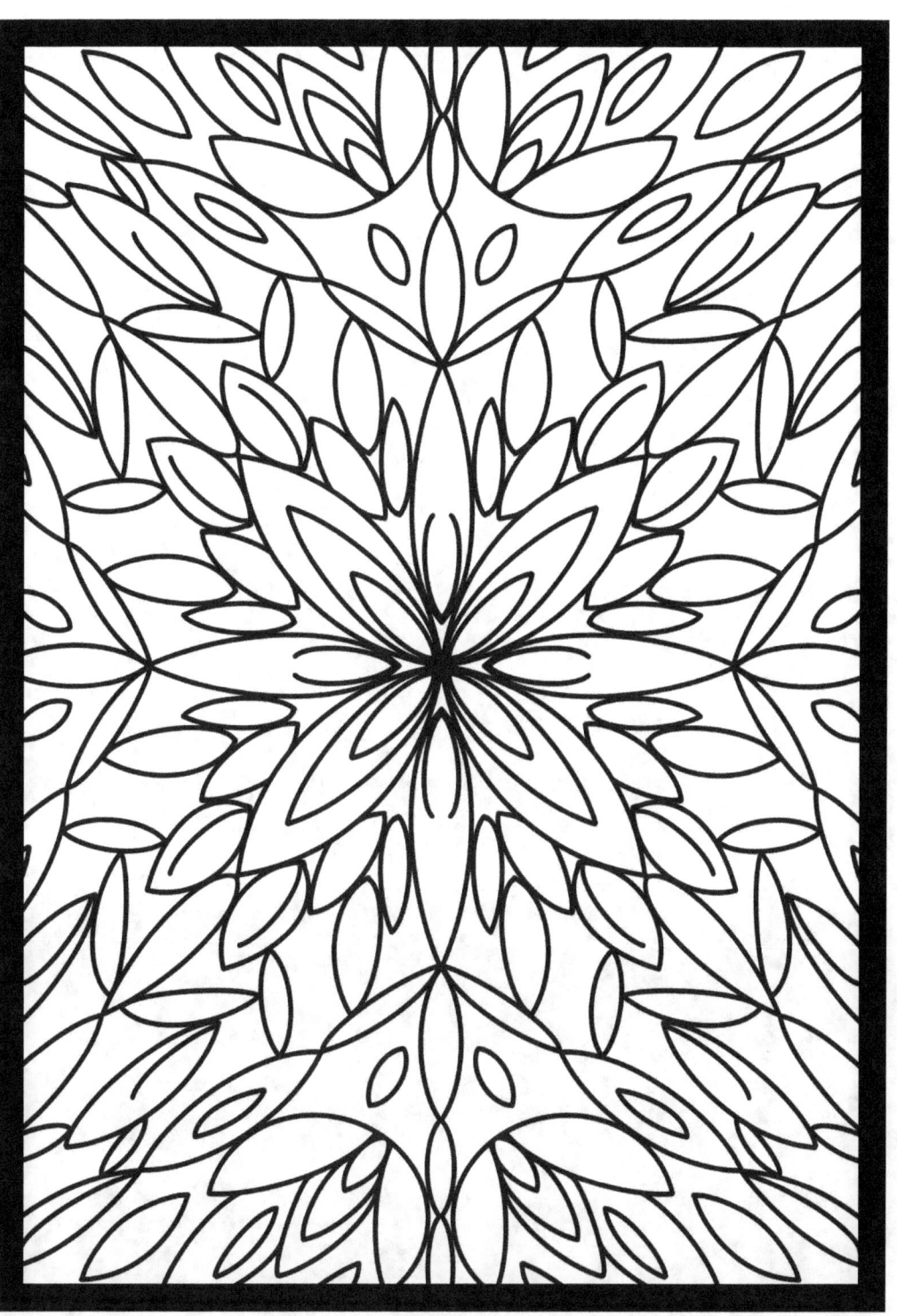

LEAVES

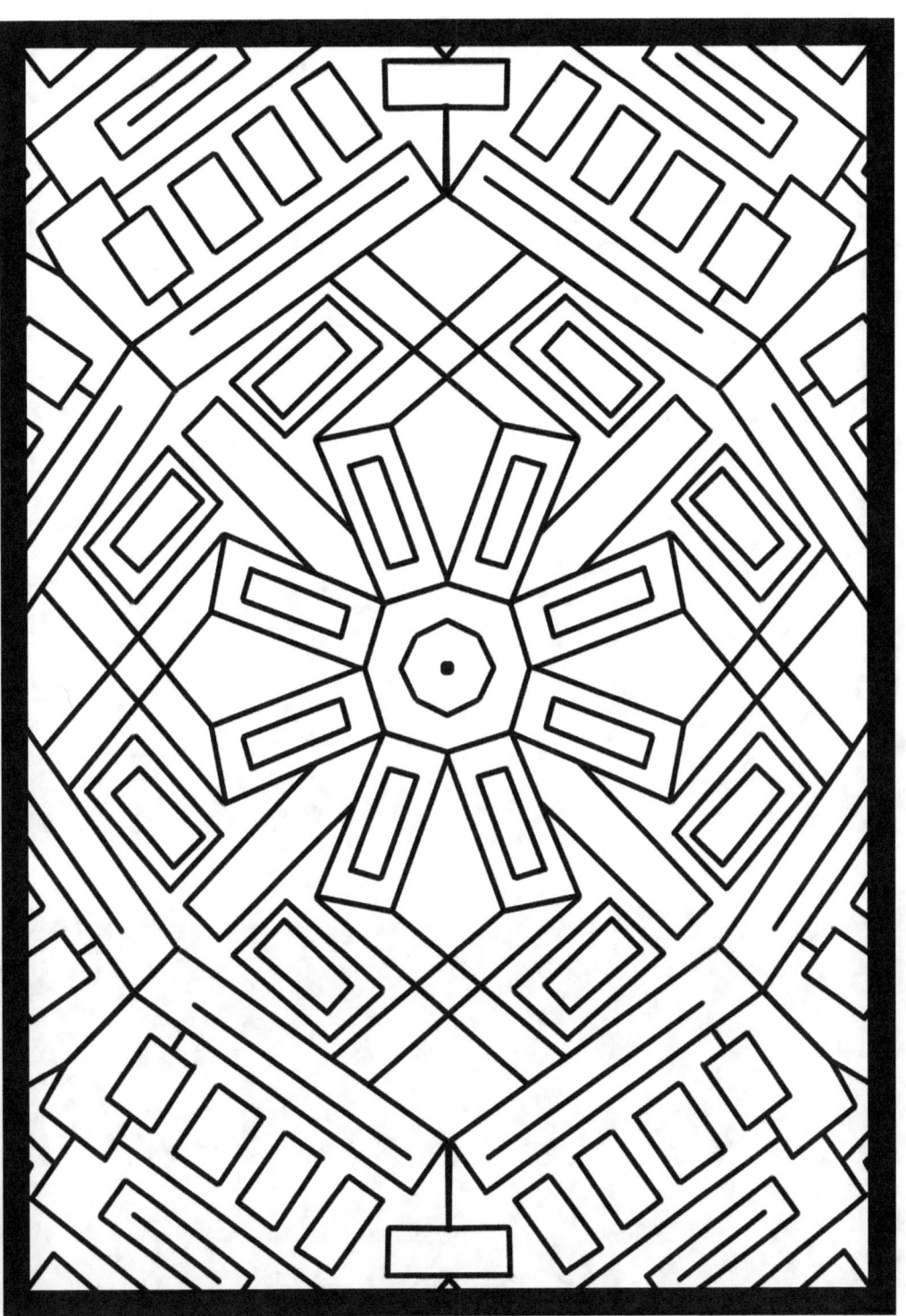

RECTANGLES

SWIRLY WHIRLY

LOVE

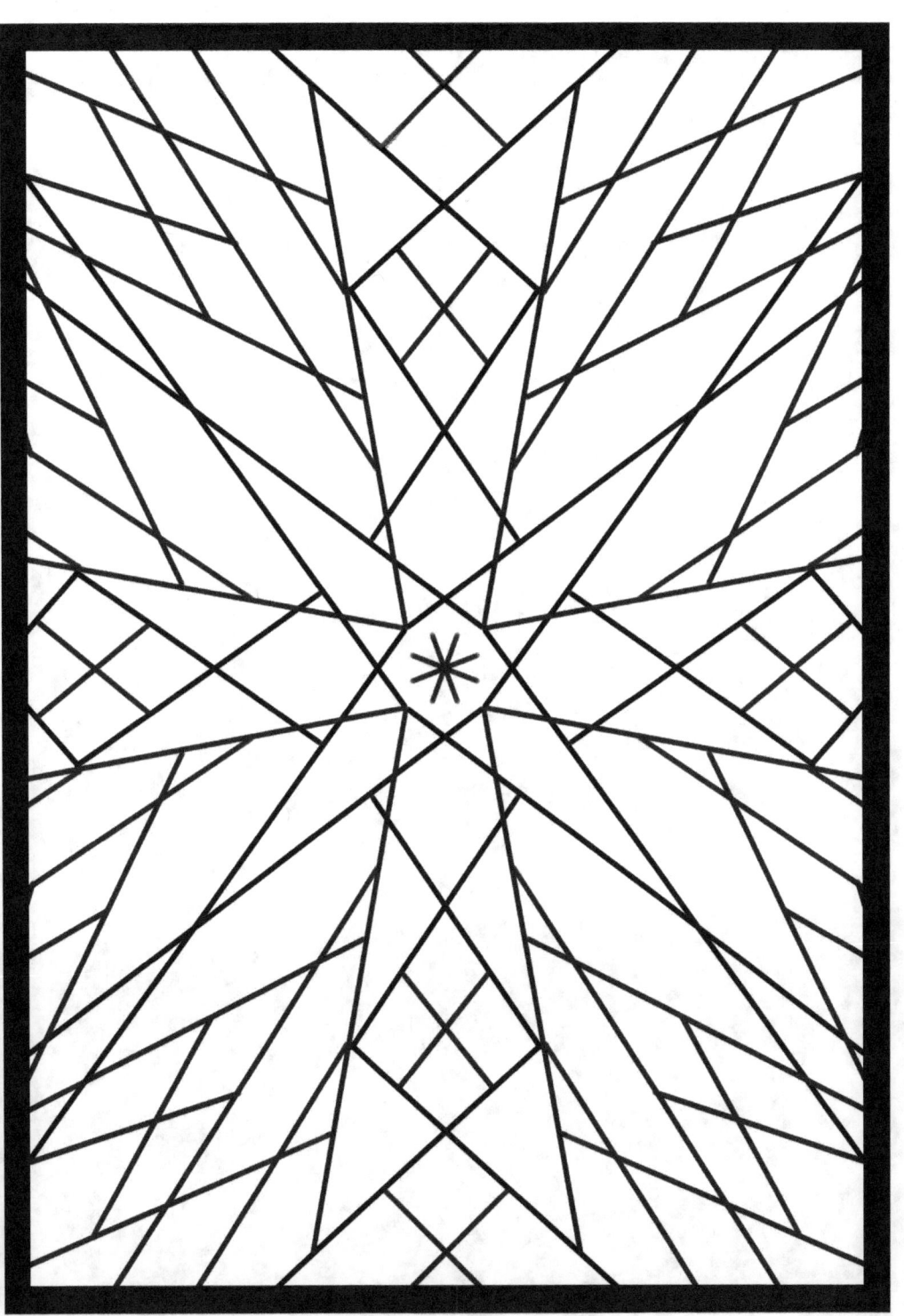

CRISSCROSS

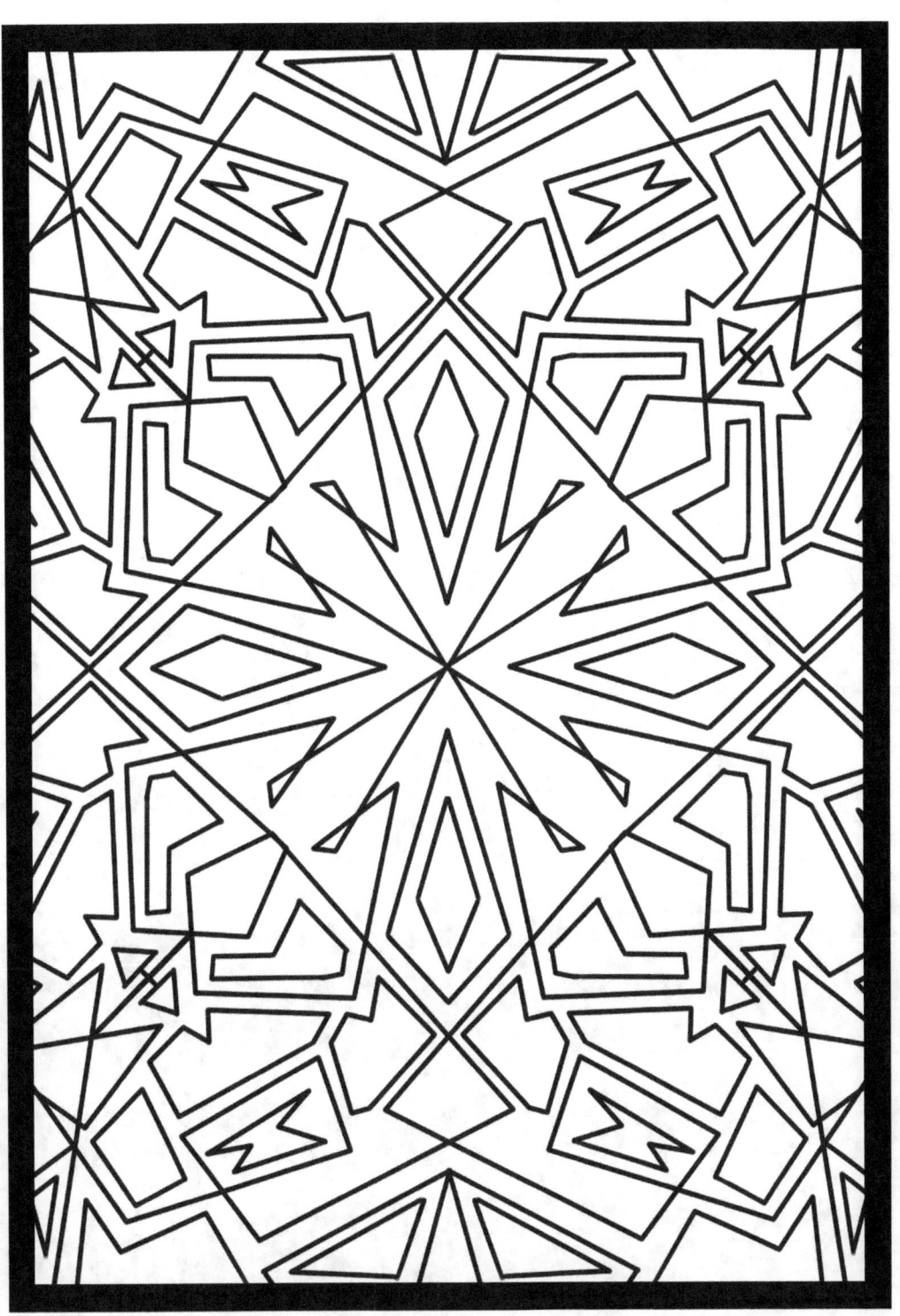

STAINED GLASS

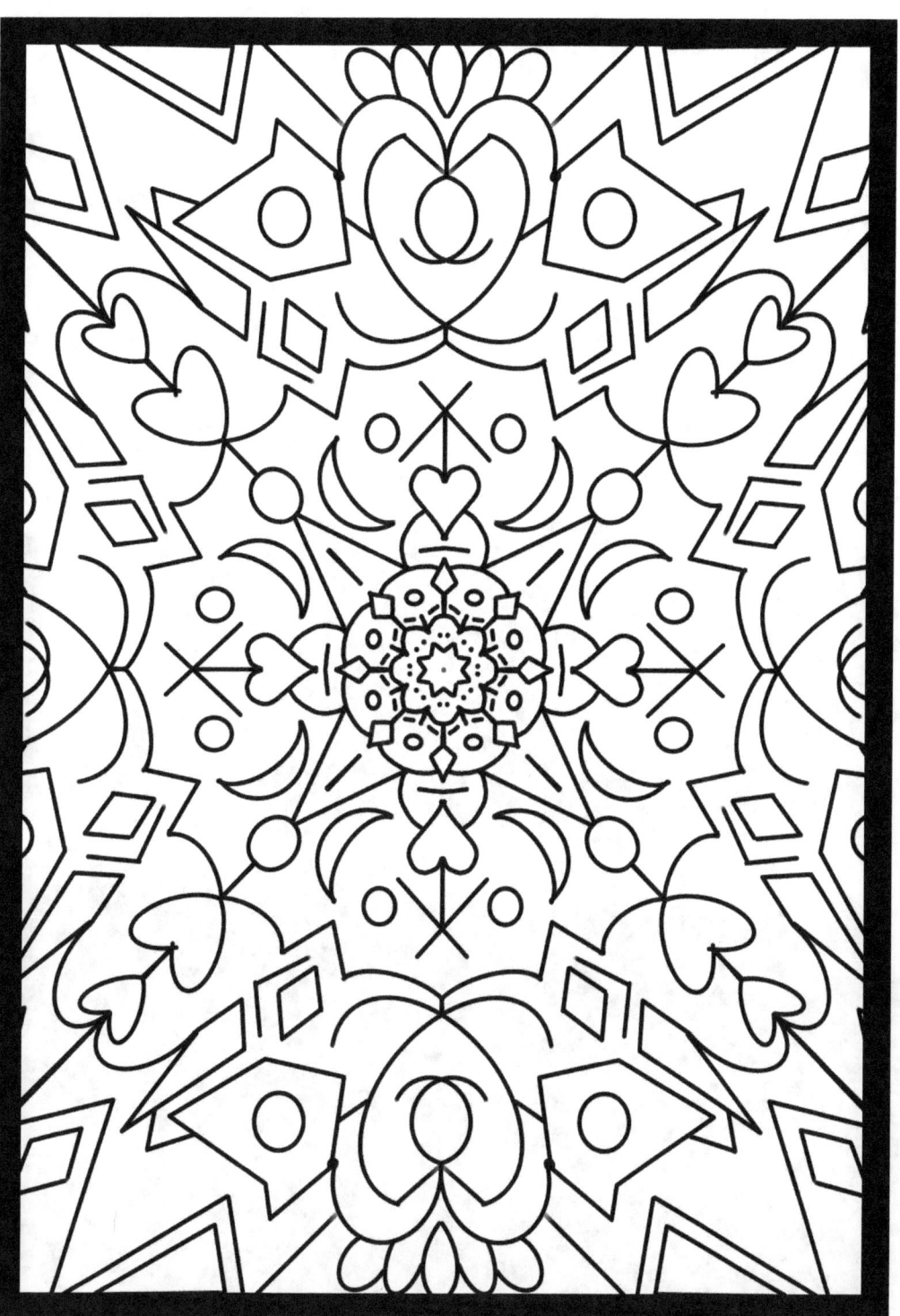

EMPRESS

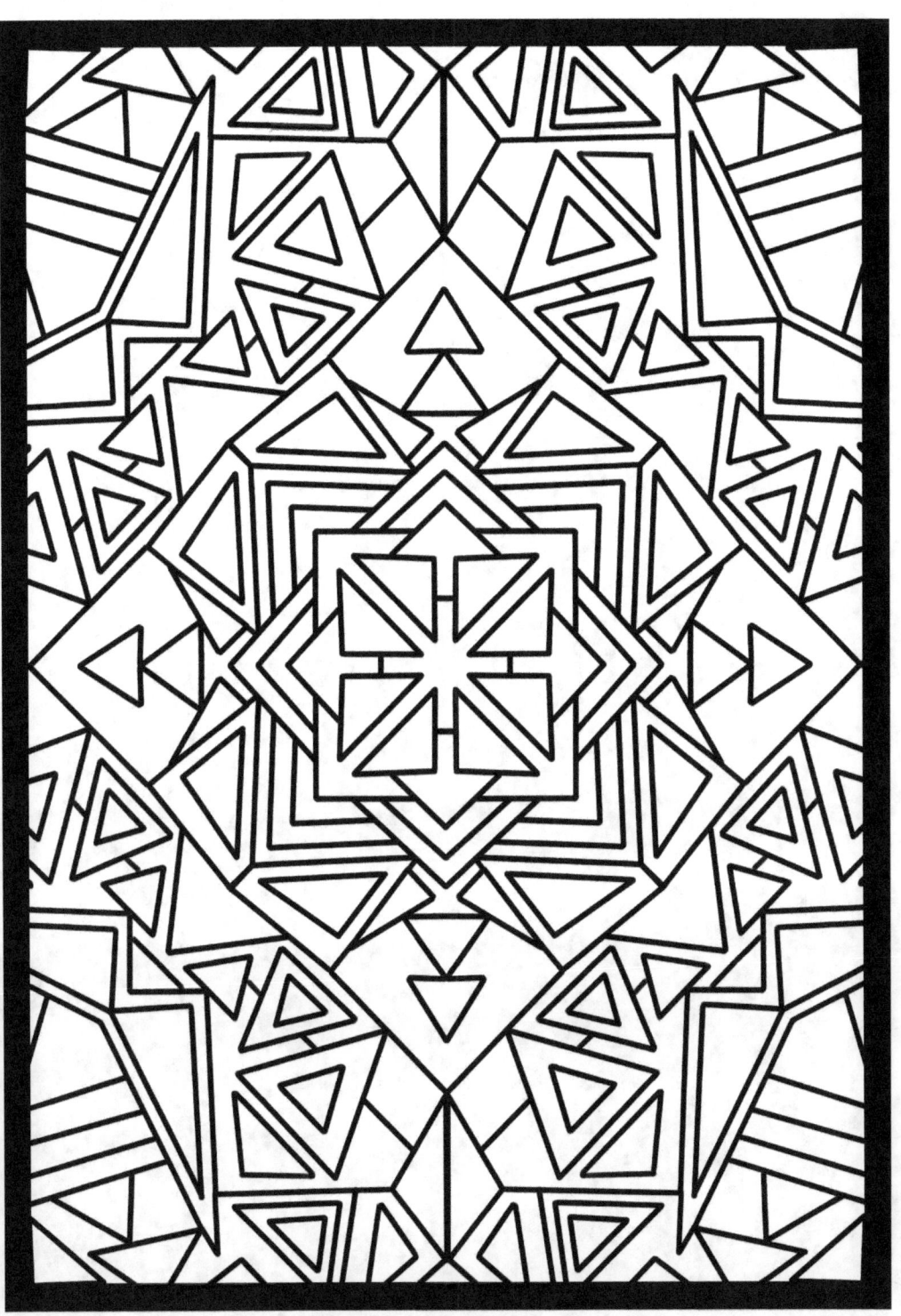

TRIANGLES

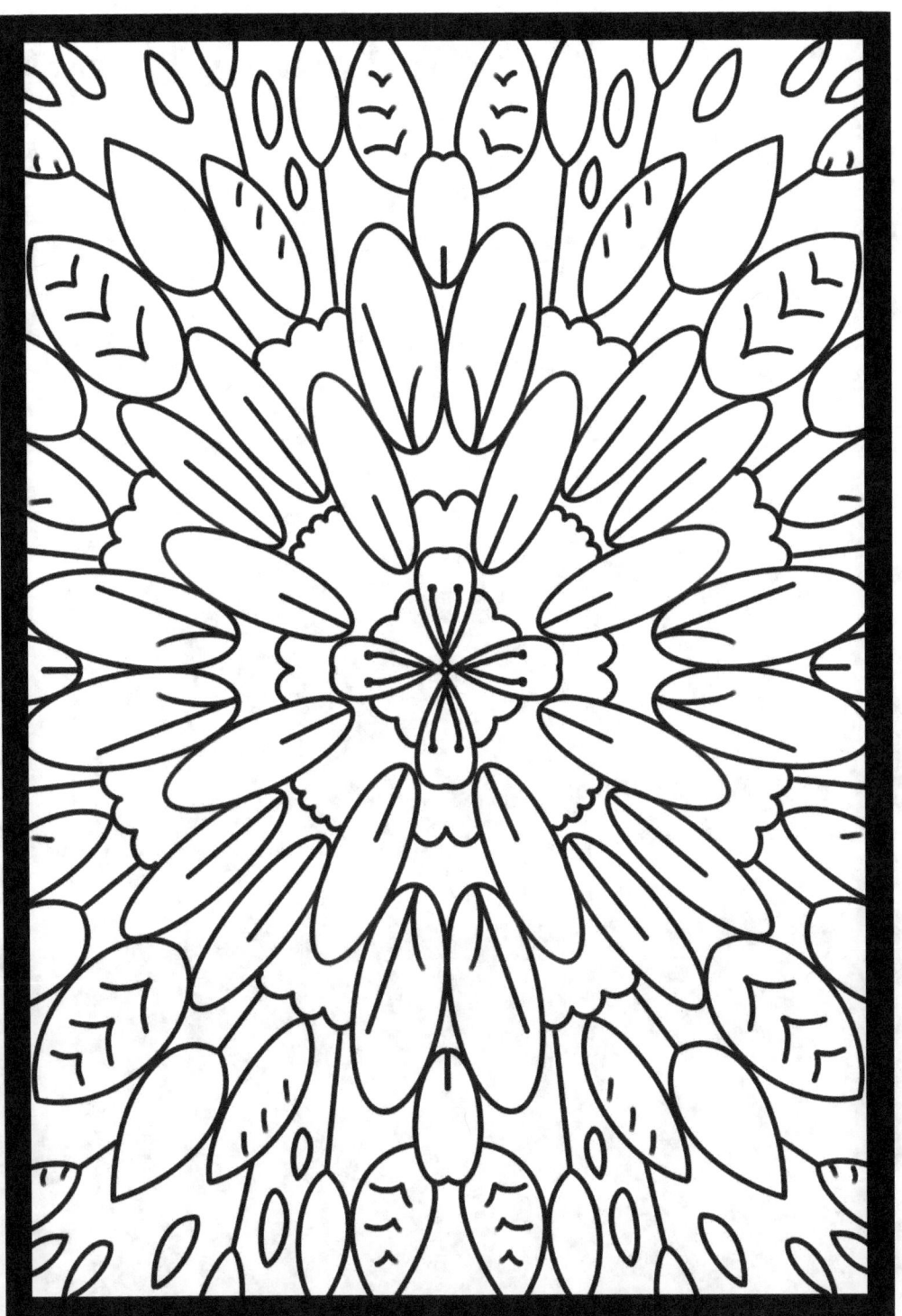

BLOOM

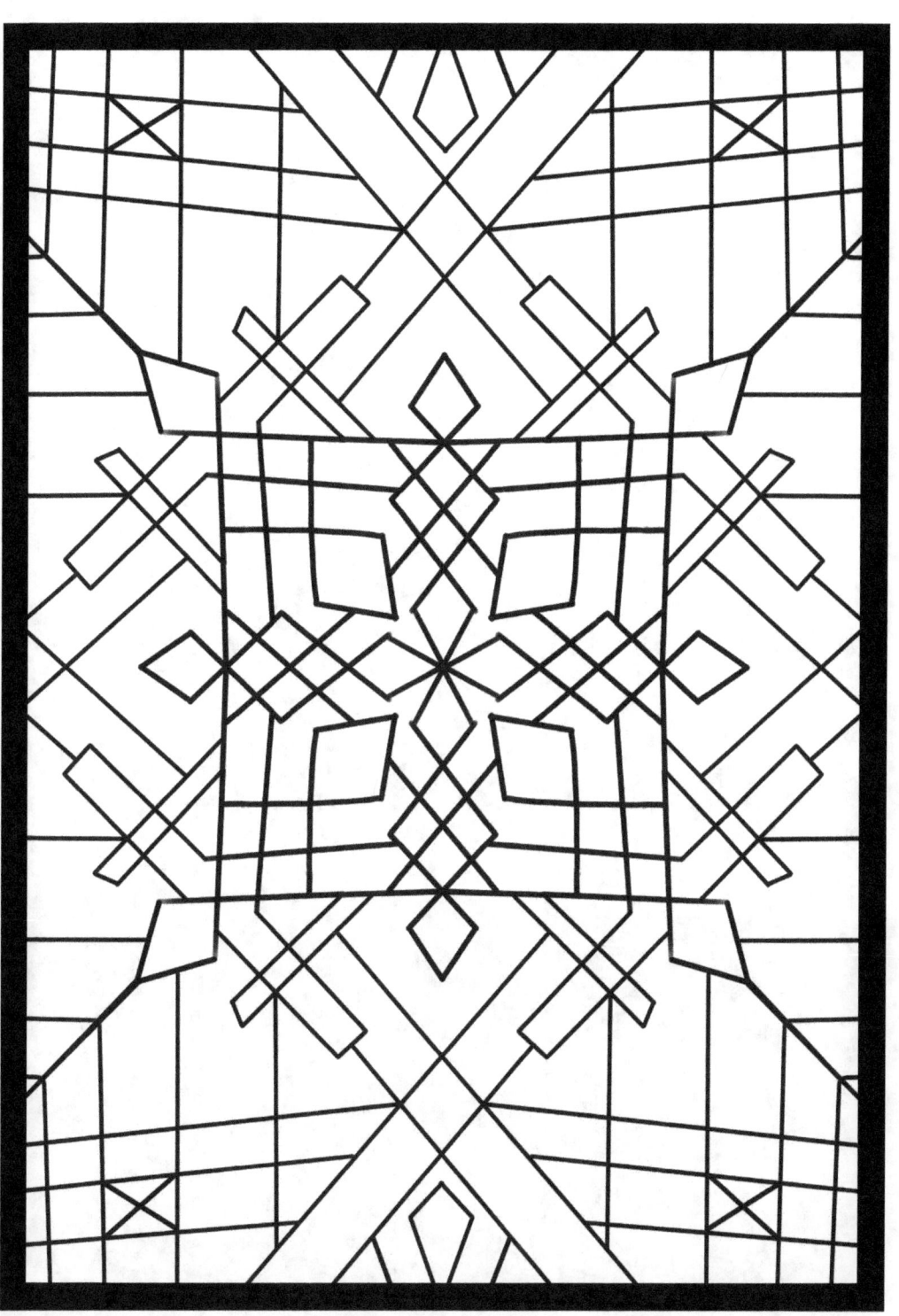

MOSAIC

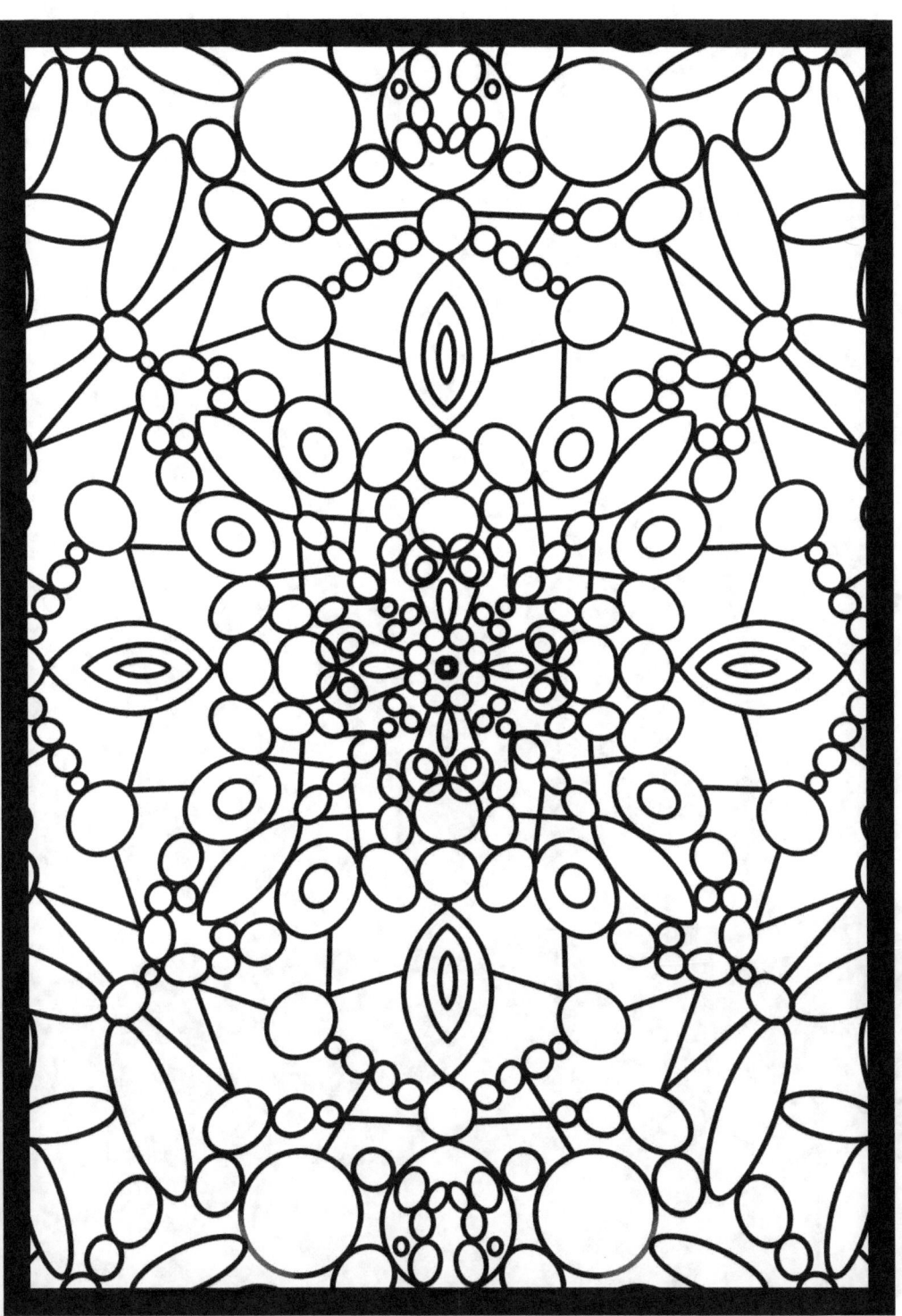

PEARLS

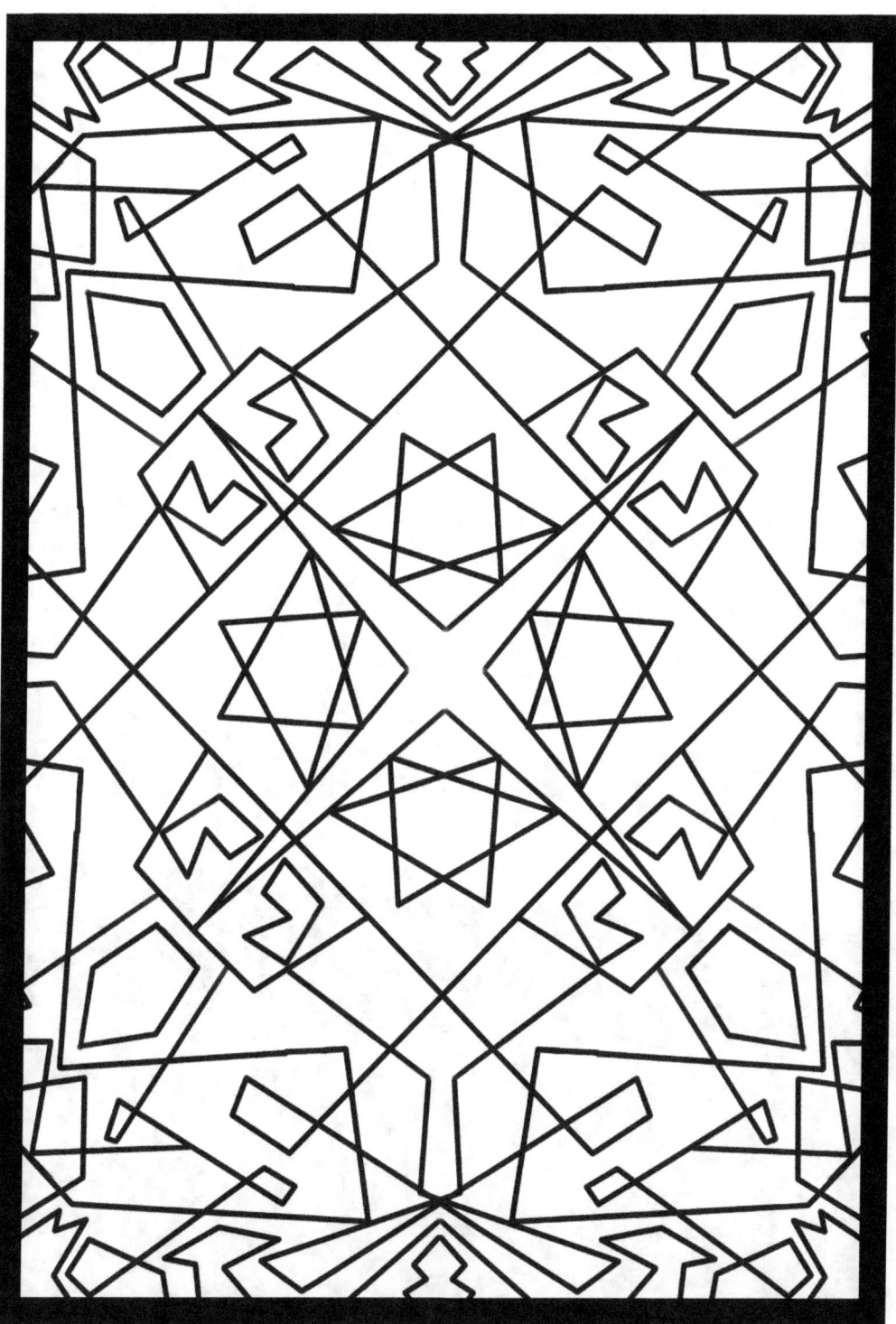

FUNK

ORNAMENTAL

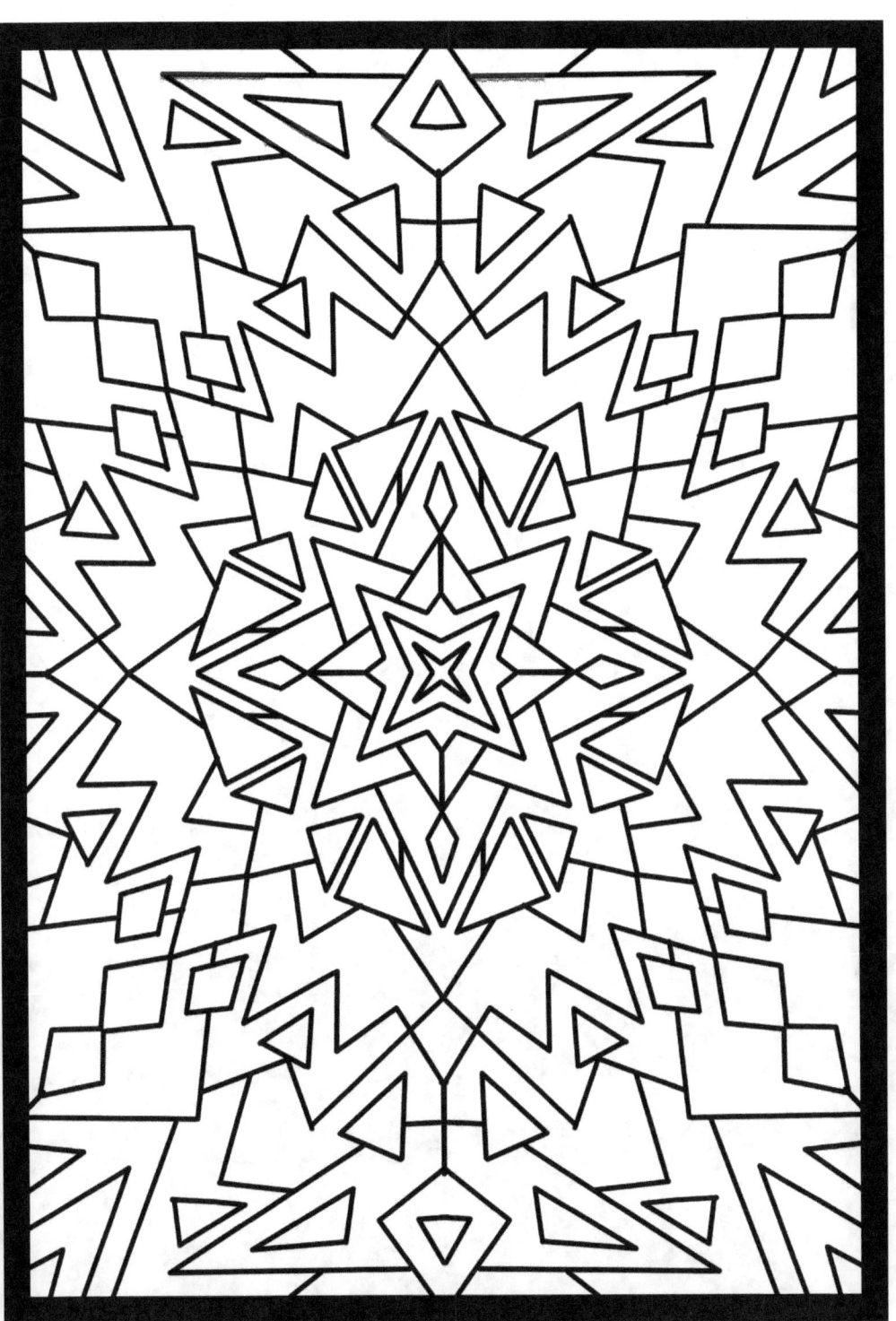
ZIGZAG

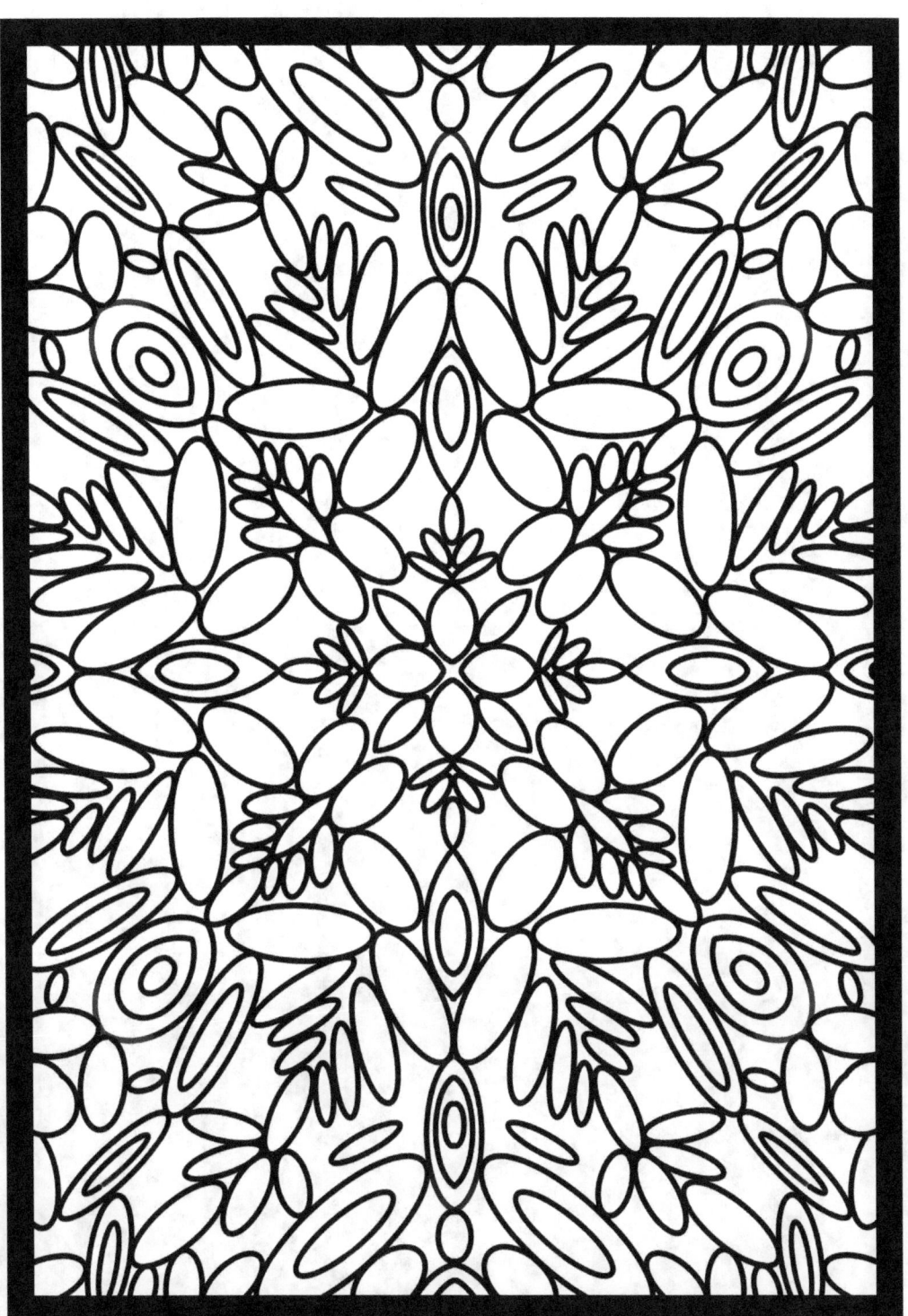

OVALS

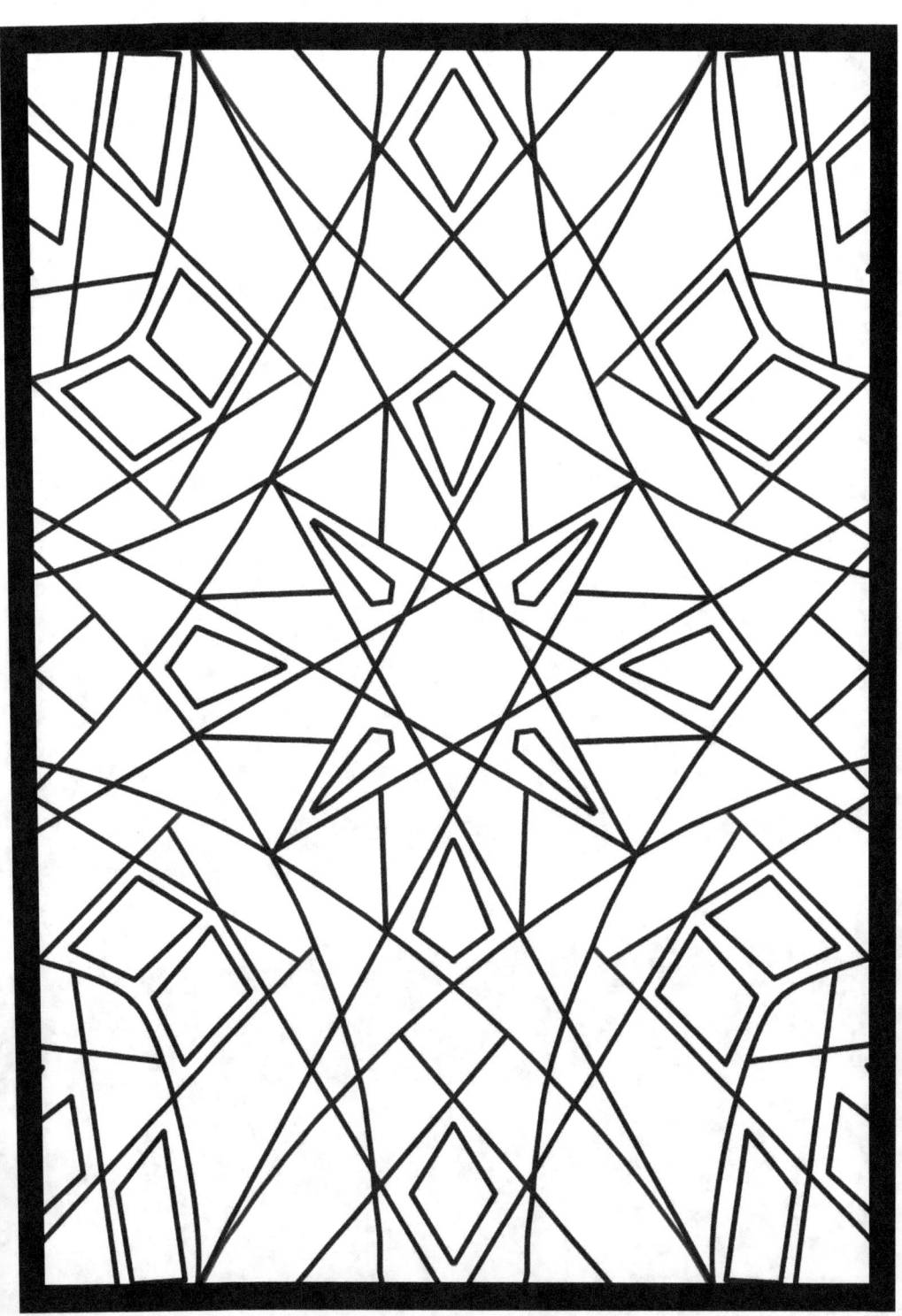
BE A STAR

www.ingramcontent.com/pod-product-compliance
Lightning Source LLC
Chambersburg PA
CBHW071122240526
45465CB00022B/777